Disorient Ballroom

Disorient Ballroom

Poems by George Uba

Turning Point

For CC
Best wishes
and sincere ~welcome
to CSUN

George Uba
-2004-

Published by Turning Point
P.O. Box 541106
Cincinnati, OH 45254-1106

Typeset in American Garamond by WordTech Communications LLC,
Cincinnati, OH

ISBN: 1932339183
LCCN: 2003109577

Poetry Editor: Kevin Walzer
Business Editor: Lori Jareo

Visit us on the web at www.turningpointbooks.com

Cover art: Maria Mami Turnmeyer
Author photo: Eric Uba

Acknowledgments

Certain poems first appeared in the following publications:

The Asian Pacific American Journal: "Suga at the Pool Hall."

Carolina Quarterly: "The Riddle."

The Jacaranda Review: "Arriving in Los Angeles, 1955."

Ploughshares: "Dawn in the Internment Camp at Heart Mountain"; "Master Oki, Keeper of Days"; "The Sanity of Tomatoes."

The Seattle Review: "Giving Up the Elements."

Southern Poetry Review: "Winchell's, 12:05 a.m."

Two Rivers Review: "As for This."

Table of Contents

—

Part 5—Giving Up the Elements

Part 6—Disorient Ballroom

Part 1:
Master Oki, Keeper of Days

Dawn in the Internment Camp at Heart Mountain

(Wyoming, 1943)

Someone clever has carved a deer
from a scrap of wood
and set it on a table or shelf
inside a shabby room among a file
of barracks, along a street of sleep.
In its miniature dawn, its hues
are gradually revealed,
its legs regain their poise,
its eyes open. Someone clever
has set a mountain in the backyard
beyond the barracks and morning's incipient din,
to loom above the density of human emotions,
to relieve the clutter of stars overhead.
And—just now it beckons to the deer.

Master Oki, Keeper of Days

1
Immigration

Master Oki played the word from its scabbard,
counted by tens, shouting the colors of decades.

Centuries are best worn with their collars showing,
he gibed. Grab time by the neck, make it speak truth

while the record plays and the money's unspent.
He crawled into a season, its leaves were damp

and humorous, though its will was benign.
The pole star flummoxed to a thousand lesser glows,

white cranes of abandonment. Slender craft,
the moon sailed six nights above Ehime.

How many villagers shall board that luminescence
tonight or the next, or the night after next?

Master Oki, please count our sturdy cousins,
lest we lose one or two in the voyage over the sea,

lest we lose their names as their faces fade
from reach. Good luck, long life, prosperity to all.

The going is rough, the sword of regret keen.
Please count them on the voyage, the voyage over.

2
Harvest

Lunging, Master Oki drove the vow home.
Its aim was true, misfortune stumbling to his knees
as the ships moved off in sturdy procession.
In that instant superstition was dispelled,
hard luck began its trek
to the Inland Sea. The villagers rejoiced.
The villagers rejoiced at the harvest
of the next 100 foreign years.

Oshiro the Immigrant:
Three Arguments and an Epilogue

1
otomodachi

Oshiro, why mull over the past
with its drapery of pain
and regret? How the cloth stinks.
How the threads pull with fatigue.

Old friend, you were poet and wanderer
by what rights, by whose say?

A wise man harvests grain
not the peccadilloes of the moon.
Any donkey can bray
at the obvious,
but the wise man pulls his load
and then some,
counts his blessings, counts his change . . .

2
tsuma

You gaze through a narrowing aperture.
The picture goes bad but you ignore it.
As if the boat still feathers the water,
and I your bride-to-be look solemnly through a frame
locking past and future into place.

Do you recall the boarding house in Brawley,
each room too narrow for the bulge of your thoughts?

The bathhouse we had to sell at a loss,
and the noodle shop on San Pedro Street
with its bland fare?

This crude world is all there is anymore.
I'll serve all five of its courses if you'll wait.

Alive, I was stronger in method and drill,
you were deeper in disobedience and urge.
(Peg and groove, not everything fits.)

You loved the fields of desert poppies at least,
where the eyes of the heart could pasture,
though your feet were tooled for flight.

3
destiny's own

Never mind the sweet petunias.
I graze on a sprig of lotus, a scrap
of peony and mustard-seed. I own the hair
of my loins, I keep my scalp in place.
The body is an unsure engine,
but my eyes still light the way.

I am Oshiro, the pauper.

My notebooks are filled with verse,
my accounts are red.
I say too much money rankles the pockets,
too much harvest deepens the debt.

Shall I strike a pose the way granite does,
shout to the four corners of success

to spread its foolish echo,
to spend its dismal coin?

At Minidoka I marked the trails of stars.
The bear led the procession of the dispossessed,
the swallow fed on wrath.
Beneath the watchful eye of a tower,
I laid siege to my captors within and without.

When I die I won't apologize.

For nothing impedes this wandering, or ever could,
my poetry in pursuit of my life.

———

Epilogue

Lately the hills of Shikoku torment my aging.
Their furry membrane of trees I wear to bed.
My dreams angle to the flight of Japanese geese,
my only children still singing above the earth.

Tomorrow, wrap me in tea leaf soaked in brine,
drape me in peach and float me downriver,
a parcel of dreams, a prophecy of salt
for the voyage to come, the splendid beginning.

Bathhouse, Kailua, 1944

He walks his son to the ofuro to scrub his back.
Steam climbs the rafters, hesitates,
seeps into the tropical night, the hint
of sugar cane harvest in the air. *Hele mai,*
Masao warns the escaping heat, water's life,
marvel of nature. The quieter of the two,
Tomasu untricks the shirt buttons with his one hand,
dispatches the belt, folds the pants along a crease
sharp as the division between yesterday and now,
and accidentally he brushes the missing limb,
its place of origin. He reports how it used to ache
where the doc stretched the skin and stitched it shut.
Claims it resembled the bound end of a sausage,
just where the wrapping pleats. But now it's smooth
and hard as the trunk of a koa tree and dimpled
at the ache. Masao leans into his grandfather tale,

the one about machetes, sugar cane,
the new foreman's toe. The son laughs
in quiet ripples, and the ripples span his face,
spilling mild reflections across the bath,
the potent air of repose. Pouring water
over the body's map, Masao routes his way
to the farewell dance his boy attended in uniform
before shipping out in a summer swell
as the Islands' garland stirred in the sea.
The depth of that night returns.
Best pals lathering, their youth intact
in Tad's loud grin after he cut the big one
and Kenny's playing with his goods
while boasting of love. What was her name?

The one Tomasu adored in silence,
poor lad. Masao rinses off,
then slides his memories into the bath
as the rest of him descends.
Round his forehead clamor beads of sweat.
The water drifts and laps. His bones ease
out of the skin's complaints.
Taking off in the Dodge, the three of them
into their separate futures. *Claire,*
he remembers now, was her name.

Tomasu's body replies to the silent bidding,
and as it does, the waters rise to Masao's neck
in a pleasurable itch. The eyes close.
Now Tad's back, and he hasn't changed.
Spent all of Italy craving Primo
and kahlua pig, and mustered out without a scratch.
Ken's re-upped with stripes,
a taste of the warrior in his mouth,
and it won't let go. And Tom,
who lied just once, at seventeen,
shipped home within a year, a medal
in place of an arm, go figure

the way she goes. It's lonely,
they tell, off Kona at night,
where the arc of the stars is earth's sole radiance,
and for once this local boy agrees.
It's talk he's good at, making the jokes
at no one's actual expense.
                              So why
you pay and pay, bleed and bleed,
when you don't hurt nobody, don't do nothing
but work your lines, weigh the fish

as the sun recedes, so long, into the wave's cold mouth,
as these Islands, turning their bellies
into the dying rays,
rinse and shine and softly bloom?

Suga at the Pool Hall

At the pool hall the boys pretend
penalty is equidistant from regret.
The books may argue this and that.
But the balls know better,
clicking approval across the spent felt,
drawing mirth while smoke keeps watch.

Suga's khakis assume their wiseguy stance,
his shirt's in commotion, full of silk
and self-regard. Six bits say
one or more of you will drop from sight,
mortally obedient to a law of significance
only your partners respect. So

what? is a good response when
your life's scheme's black as an 8-ball,
black and slick as a tide of hair,
or when it's your round heart
forever teetering on the brink.
Still, it's coming, that day

when some punk reappears,
toting a grudge with live ammunition.
He's coming. And beneath his jacket,
inside a corner of that cheap vest,
or angled off some slick side pocket,
he'll be holding the last laugh.

The Burden of Happiness

America, hold my place in line.
Just now I saw my grandfather's ghost
working produce in a *yaoya* on Jefferson.
Outside, the P-car rattles its dusty sermon
along the mind's provincial tracks.

Old man who made the apples squeak,
who put lettuce leaves on notice,
gave carrots erections to this day,

I want to ask your opinion
of navel oranges, laxatives,
and why heaven's trail looks so faint.
Is it just the smudge of progress?
Or something less scientific?

About humiliation.
How many courses did they serve,
the uniformed agents of the state?
If longevity shortened is levity,
why is history so grim
a mortician?

My idea is to unturn stones
and communicate in zen.
Why should converts have all the advantage?
Let's break the back of unending toil
you paid the god-of-getting-ahead. Love
was not a word you used, and so what?
Sweat was sufficient.
And so was fortitude.

If we children were cause, as Mother says,
I forgive her anyway.
I strew salt on the past
to preserve its injury,
to sharpen its sting.

And I accept the burden of happiness
on this the tenth day of the fifth month
of the rest of my stay in this visible empire of ash.
Whosoever is crushed by sacrifice,
I am telling you, America,
you do not see my heartbreaking ghost.

Part 2:
Family Album

Family Album

To the one that solved the riddle, thanks.

This is me at seven in the wool shorts and jacket.
My mother is so pretty and does not look mad
at anyone. Bryan boasts the odd bow tie,
the first of countless accessories
calculated to set him apart

and keep him there. Laura sits unnoticed
in the grip of someone's arm
because she is my sister and a girl.
My shorts are navy and they itch.

Maybe that's why my eyes blink when the flash pops.
Or maybe there's something I don't care to see.

And the one, the one with the large hands,
with his mouth shut,
must be come hell or high water my dad.

The Atmosphere of Learning
in Waynesville

(Missouri, 1954)

Begin with the company of cows,
their disorderly calm.
A neighborly stink climbs the knoll
in late spring, with the children, to school.
In the distance the Ozarks approach or recede.
It's difficult to say from where the bus grinds off.

A child waits on the teeter-totter.
This and the dismal swings
are the furniture of the place,
its cooperating spirit
the meager dirt yard
the marbles spread across.
Grasshoppers stretch their legs in the heat.
A boy named Tim catches one mid-boast.
Feeds it to his grin.

Tall and stern, the schoolhouse windows warn
where the fun stops, where anger lurks,
red in the face. Once I am punished
for talking in class, and the paddle appears
along with the scowl. I bawl so hard
he lets me off with only a scolding
stitched across my rear. *Lucky you*, he sniffs.
I practice my capitals: "F" goes with "Fear"
as "G" with "God."
I open my arithmetic and read its lies.
I know that one is greater than thirty.

That two times two means more misfortune
than I care to commit.

They say children are colorblind.
The answer to that one is False.
A born leader, Judy Schlinker gauges my skin,
the others noticing its somber hue.
I do not register its flaws.
I tell them I live on the army post
miles away, where recruits drill in the sun.

The day I step in the pile of cowshit,
tracking it into class,
I puzzle over the rich odor of decay,
until, glancing down, I observe the offending shoe.
She is miles away, this week's substitute,
in a heightened state of inattention.
So I wipe my humiliation off
on the metal runner of my desk.

For two weeks it stays there, undisturbed.
Gradually it hardens and dries,
leaking its wanton aroma
into the atmosphere
of learning in Waynesville.

Arriving in Los Angeles, 1955

It's warm in the sunny little town.
The palm trees lean toward us,
full of neighborly advice.
People are busy
minding their own business.
Zinnias bloom. There's only one freeway
I know of, one gas station
with mustard pumps shaped like domes.
This is nice, a confidential life.
There's no school yet, no lack of friends,
just the shiny buttons
on my father's uniform, miniaturized suns
repeating the word "army" for the last time.
When we haul out the new Buick
with the California plates,
there's a plucky song to sing to on the radio.
How happy we are, our family, how the fleeing
landscape's recalled in the form of plenty.
At the beach the men will be pale & shirtless,
what a funny sight they'll make,
my father & uncles, everyone smiling,
everyone happy to be alive. *Dad,*
pay attention, my son calls out
from the back seat.
Of course he doesn't really say that.
He's too young to talk that way,
he's not even born yet.
That's the thought of him napping in back.
"Wake up, wake up, son.
That's me, that's your dad
when he was young." But still he sleeps on,

his lower lip adrift,
his eyelids clasped shut. Tomorrow
is years away.

The Threat of Canned Spinach

The spinach hints of dank colors and khaki moods.
I watch it watching me in its shallow bowl of waiting.
I won't fight it with a teacher patrolling the cafeteria,
his arms folded and alert like two sticks of lit authority.
A single soppy leaf is enough to make me retch.
A gun butt folds my chest in half, my heart left battered
and bent, its signals enfeebled, *mayday, mayday*.
They must load a lot of roughage in a single round.
So it must be good for it to taste so bad and for me
to swallow it daily along with homework and math.
I can't leave my seat for the playground,
where I could lurk beneath some gentler leaves.
I can't go toilet or talk to my neighbors on either side
until I'm done, that's a rule. That's a rule I've learned
at this latest new school, where all I know is how to shut up
like crazy. I watch it watching me, set to explode.
My fork reaches out. Takes another stab at obedience.
This time I miss. Thank God. I'm not dead yet.

Finding the Word

Find the first harsh word I used.
It's about. Keep looking. Fetch the wagon

if it's too big. Take this loop.
It's to catch the bite before it strikes.
Now stand it in the corner
for the penalty phase. You may read silently,
but don't pick your nose or chew the wax plum,
and of course don't play with yourself

for the time being. Look, it squirms
like moss in a swamp, cowers like fur
on a spent hare, not so tough now.
Take that, and I'll call it love.

If that lesson's in error,
I'll blame a misbegotten theory.

Now you are almost grown.
The wise guy is finally me.
Here is the word off its hanger,
here the word stretched out.
The word is *son*. Please
see if it fits. Then pass it on.

What He Forgot to Mention
the Last Time They Spoke

*

She's spoiling for a fight.
Dad, he could have been a sailor
stoutly facing the oncoming gale
instead of a dentist
skirting the dangers of the domicile
by repeating his mantra—
"ahhhh."

*

A son writes his first apology at seven.
On a 3 X 5 lined index card
he leaves on the hallway door.
The next morning the card
has found its way back
to his nightstand. A father's forgiveness.
Now he understands the miracle of writing.
Later he leaves a similar card for her.
He never sees it again.
He knows this is not the difference
between fathers and mothers
but a lesson in penmanship.

*

Deliberately, he stores his voice
in his bureau, herds its obstreperous
retorts into the convincing dark.

Sleep, oh beauties. Amid socks
and gentlest underwear.
When anger rages down the hall,
remember, you are only dreaming.

*

She becomes a Republican.
FDR, after all, put her in camp.
At war's end, she addresses a banquet
of white ladies. She supported FDR,
she declares. After all,
"first we had to win the war."

*

She tells him stories of the 442nd.
He pictures the assault at Anzio,
the frozen battlefield of Boulogne.
The bravery of nisei. Loyal Americans.
She complains of a date she had
years before, the man who called her
a cold fish. It rankles. The false label.
This time she is right, undoubtedly.
She is not cold. *Bakatare!* She is afraid.

*

They leave the stingy Italian landlord
on the Southside for a suburb up north.
For weeks she tracks leads.
Finally, a realtor who sells to Orientals.
A charming 3-BR Brick Two-Story.
In front of it stretches a vast cemetery.

To the side, a cinder alley
parallels a second cemetery.
He hates his new school. He loves his house.

*

Her anger is a second cancer.
The first strikes in her thirties.
Strikes her breast, her lymph nodes.
Back then she has a 5% chance.
Already to the doctors she is
a grim statistic. They will grow up
motherless, her little ones,
just as she had done.
Miraculously, she survives.
With each recurrence she battles
to teach them more self-denial, more chores.
Always to her desperate timetable. Once,
taking his usual list of chores
to her bedside, he makes a mistake
he never repeats. He calls her lazy.

*

One night his aunt comes over
to check his manners. They look good
from here. If they were an apple,
you could call them polished.
If they were reducible to one word,
you could call them articulate.
You could say they match her mink.
Rushing over to him, she whispers,
try to be good to your mother!
Her perfume is glamorous,

but he scarcely notices. So
her sister knows, the whole bleeding
planet knows the family secret:
he is a rotten human being.

*

There's no question
the blank page of his jaw
is asking for a slap
to be drawn across it.
A hand obliges. It stings
insufficiently and fails
to produce the desired image
of cooperation. She
experiments with wood paddles,
including one with geometric
holes designed to spread
obedience concentrically.
It hurts, but his skin's
thicker than he thought.
His tears flow insincerely.
The marriage of
art and science has failed.

*

Friday
she resumes talking to him.
Which means she is ready to accept his apology.
So here goes, and not just for television privileges
after three days of going without.
His bad habit is,
he can never remember

what they fought about. So
he is repentant. But vague.
Why must she always say,
"Do you know what you did wrong?"
Finally, she gives him the correct answer,
which sounds plausible,
as even the wrong ones do
on the multiple choice tests
we kids call "multiple guess."

*

This year he vows will be different.
He promises himself
a girlfriend by Christmas.
Meanwhile he lives out his fantasy in the john.
Until one day he notices the pictures
he's kept stashed in the garage
have stood up on the long verticals of their legs
and walked out of his plan.
But still when he's in the bathroom,
he expects that voice: *what's taking so long,*
come on out of there.

*

She hates it when he bolts out of the house
after all the screaming, the night
swallowing him as it does the birds.
She forbids him to go. But he goes.
She is afraid that in a rage he'll fling himself
from a cliff or in front of a speeding car.
(She denies this but it is true.)
But he would never do that, no.

He is just walking. Walking his anger
at night, the way others walk their dogs.
Well, not quite. It's more like
taxiing down a runway,
gathering speed and momentum,
learning the take-off, before the flight.

*

She will die soon.
It will be all his fault.
He knows because she told him this
many times over the years.
All. Your. Fault.
He used to believe her.
Today it is not a matter
of belief or blame.
Or even forgiveness.
No need to parry
those lancing words.
No reason to shield
a grown man.
She lived.
That's enough.

*

She fed him good values
on the wrong tray.
The widower could not eat in English.
He was sinewy, taut as rope,
and he bound his children in a knot
of survival through the Depression.
He could live off pine nuts and bitterroot

long before the government
closed in on his skin color,
long before he lined up for the words
messu haru, and long long before
he became the smiling grandpa.

*

She didn't have a mother.
Her constant refrain when criticism
threatened to cloud her horizon.
The formula was simple, to be sure.
Reduce all other exigencies
to the one brutal fact.
But he learned to do more than agree,
unfurling her preoccupation
like a wounded umbrella,
its ribs like spikes,
and hoisting it above,
a shield from what she didn't have,
acknowledgement for what he did.

On the Political Nature of Divorce

Suppose divorce is a map gone bad. If you had every advantage,
as your parents agreed, why didn't you take the prescribed route?

You watch it unfold. You follow the arrows, clearly marked.
Along the way things happen—roadwork, mishaps, inclement
        weather—

but you pick your time, your place, and you start again. Whoops,
and you start again. You put your finger to the map

and trace its line like a raised ridge along the skin. That's it,
it's a kind of scar, but you remember it and that's how you learn

to find your way, your parents agreed. Suppose they were right
in blaming you 100%. It's not logical, but just suppose.

Considering all they went through, and *they* stayed put.
You could point to the number of squiggly lines materializing

on your map. Squiggly and impertinent. Plus the eyes are bad.
Half the time you don't see where you're going. The other half

is worse: you're sure you do. But supposing they were right,
you still owned a different map. Theirs was a map of America

from sea to shining sea. Yours was a map of *you* in America,
of the alien and the alien nation.

Part 3: Critique

Critique

A Life (1977)

The floor hosts clots of blood,
a trace of stool. Hurry lurks

in the buckled sheet, the slide
of attendants through the door.

This morning's wordless rush
had kept a stillness borrowed

from dozing streets intact.
Our way seemed lit by candles

braced to expire at dawn's
exhaling wish. We made one too,

remake it now. Close my eyes,
it's close to love. I mean

the moans at intervals,
their mounting toward

a finish love wants
to reach but not reach

too fast. But want aside,
my eyes aren't shut,

their minor task to heed
the strain that twists your face

as hands arrive, scrubbed and
ably gloved. Hold on. Repeats

prevailing calm. But hold it,
HOLD IT! is a furiouser blast,

stark as vengeance. Urgency
drives you, knot or blade,

beyond control. Endurance stretched,
at last snaps. The room tilts

its bowl of concentration
and then—

the final push and push and give us
one more big—and there

the hairy scalp
spills into reach (got it!)

and the rest covered with mucous,
blood, umbilicus. They snip

and suction rapidly,
discount the shock of division

but not the clawing for air.
Exhausted, struggling with afterbirth,

you don't hear what
we do—clamor of silence.

Outside, the a.m. traffic
revs, heeling sparkles

off the asphalt's skin,
and fills a space. Until a sound,

not breath exactly,
intervenes. Pause. Faintly.

The lungs beat hollowly
in their invisible drum.

Rasp.

Perhaps an idea is born:
not relief but repetition,

not the uncanny cry,
a swaddling, and the pan

of warmth beneath a lamp,
but misery in its ceaseless

tug. The body, torn
from the close wet comfort

of dark, the oceanic canal,
haunts the brutal light.

*   *   *

He's what is called a strider.
To put a name on it conceals alarm.

They've arranged the transfer
to a larger place. Another *facility*,

which can mean *with ease.*
Or neo-natal specialists and infant ICU.

I've seen the shriveled leg
as sign of more to come.

A social worker greets us,
performing duty for the State. No,

when I finally catch the drift,
we're not on welfare.

2
Visitation

        The lacy clouds they might appliqué

to such stark walls
        have drifted off

to distant Zanzibar.
           A nightstand demands

a bud vase, greeting card, stuffed bear.

        Except there is no nightstand.

    Nor tropic latitude to this belt of cold.

Only exile
        wonder
            like an untried

    mobile

       floating below its ceiling

        of suspense.

"Stay as long as you like."

    Unconditional, the offer fills

       a self-staging I start feeding from:

that somehow this is my own

life's drama.

My eyes pose danger on the freeway,

but roadwork persists.

Missing spleen,

damaged heart, inverted

kidney—

the bad news pours in

the way concrete molds

fill with intent to solidify.

It's only a matter of time.

Which is what materializes
in abrupt abundance.

On the Saturday he is four days old

ABC features Stanford vs. San Jose,

a football telecast I still recall
for no reason

except that waiting is a game

within the game, whatever the stakes,

however determinable

the outcome.
    Three hours later,
         one fate is sealed.

      A nurse's

  silence   invites me in.

The doctors rule the intercom.

  I stand guard beside ventilator, heart monitor,

    and other engines of medical concern.

  His pulse so tiny I could clasp him whole

    in two palms. I try.
        His own hand replies—

fingers curling instinctively around my own,

but gently, experimentally, as if testing

      an unexpected bone with the tongue
  of his grasp.

  I feel the hard steadfastness

of fingernails. Take their pink into my heart.

  The ventilator flutes his underlip,

which inherits an open sore.

                              I ease

the offender to one side,

                         and he reacts.

One eye widening with the movement resembles

              the bright, black dot of a question mark.

The other stays half-closed, devotionally.

          Yes, I pray then. Who wouldn't? Pity him

    God   this little boy.

                 That's the substance,

I forget the form.   Maybe I nourish

          that flesh momentarily with my daily,

now nightly, visits, inkling grief.

                    Maybe not. No. Definitely no.

I wonder: how can I retrieve

                    three stolen hours?

3
Waiting

Your mother reminds me of a bird. Chatty
and confiding, increasingly garrulous,
she flits from daughter to daughter to daughter,

house by house, as if chitchat offered genuine food
for thought. Now she arrives saying nothing
but busying herself in the anxious kitchen,

where we expect the call, the muted voice
announcing, it's over, please come down,

please. I admire her altered habit. How
she drops the rag of silliness she's worn

and faces death unflinchingly. Her talk
is somber, realistic, all about gravesites
and mortuaries. I'm sent to scout out

granite markers—size, script, message, design.
As always, you have little to say. Your
stitches must ache, but you don't let on.

You eat little. Wash clothes.
Hold and bathe our girl,
precocious and sweet.

I fill you in,
though you never ask, on the latest.

You must want this over, as I do, ·
for his sake. But you never
confide in me, or anyone. Television

flickers across our bed, its lies
intact, almost necessary.

It's not important to believe
but to occupy time, which,
like space, means neither good nor ill
to any of us. Least of all are words,

you feel, because they change nothing,
make no bit of difference. Later

I'll rage at the cardiologist
who returns none of my calls. Why

won't you agree with my anger, acknowledge
the legitimacy of its claim, its source's
mutual wound? Because, your silence says,

it makes no difference. Your sister calls

repeatedly, wanting your mother on some trivial
this or that. Can't she see
(how can she not?) that each ring

cuts brutally across the nerves? Finally,
at my repeated prompting, you ask her
not to call. Why am I
guilty for this request?

Again I've got it wrong.
Because it makes no difference.

At last I begin to see: I think of all of us
in this together, of suffering as a kind
of kin, of him as an extension of us,
of language as our bond, while you think,
let us say, more purely of him. Already

you have let go, let him to be himself alone
in his living and dying
in a gesture neither kind nor unkind
but in a gaze more steady than I can bear.

His condition worsens. Visiting him,
we encounter the aftermath of war.
So many inexplicable wounds, such blank
confusion. I recognize the world in him.

You see but him.

4
Fractures from a Future

Today from my apartment balcony I hear people
conversing, cars accelerating, the silly
tune sung by the catering truck as it slides
into its space behind the dry cleaners
I keep meaning to try. November
was the last time I tried to write this poem.

I saw Aunt Lillian the other day. For years
I didn't know she suffered from narcolepsy.

Now her back's bowed from osteoporosis,
so that in her aging she's lost three inches

or more. Holding her fragility to me
for a moment, I recalled how she offered her

own humble embrace that long ago Christmas
instead, she thought, of comfort.

"I'm bad with words," she whispered
brokenly, seeking forgiveness.

As if believing her sorrow were not
sorrow enough. Dear Aunt,

yours are the only words
I still recall. . .

Today your cousin's wife lies dying of cancer,
too young and proof again of an adage.
I think you still have not called her, have you?

You're not callous. But remain protected
in the sense of distance your convictions
permit. You'll never change. . .

Today, can you see beyond my provoking silences
in those final years together, beyond the self-
consuming chores you divide the days into

like zodiacal zones? You bearing
water to the stovetop or to the panting dog
know contentment of sorts. It's a
scrupulous assurance, this cause and effect.

And now I'm gone, no tiresome demands
are made on anyone. Even the dishes are easier
done by yourself or—why not?—strewn in piles.

5
Day Eight

and with the call we broke
through each other's distance we rode

that intolerable crest to the bedside
I amazed at how the warmth still penetrated

the flesh as if the flesh prevailed
and holding that warmth rocking it

to the kuck kuck kuck of the second hand
and here your turn to to and fro to and fro

your lovely son undamaged and new
and rendered immaculate beneath this

disease of time here I'll just I'll just
and you are stricken

your father guides his granddaughter
silently through the

lobby she won't remember any
of this that's a blessing

my parents were here before us
here when he died thank goodness

he wasn't alone he's not suffering now
and the next day

my mother phones she says dad cried
in bed I've never seen him cry

nor has she but I can see it
at this instant my father of reason

plunging without aid of net
into morning's incomprehensible abyss. . .

6
Father and Child

Your father could not wade through this
interminable morass. I see him standing apart,

shoulders hunched, his mechanic's hands wanting
tearful faucets or a gate's shattered latch

to fix. I know what those hands would say
if they could speak, I know the eloquence

of their daily tasks. But it's not enough,
labor. Not enough, silence, shyness, reserve.

Nor naked good will, when a world abruptly
tilts on its axis, slips and falls away

with a cry. Puzzled, then angry, I could not
fathom why he never uttered a word of

comfort or once (not once!) held or touched you
in your grief. And why you didn't mind.

So alike the two of you—uncomfortable
among strangers, among family

placid as a shoe. But that's it, isn't it?
You see the inadequacy of his response,

of love alone. But you've never heard words
that helped, that consoled, that mattered either.

So why bother? Only actions speak, or fail to, in your experience. The rest is silence.

7
Search and Repair

The funeral—no. Just say it was brief,
private. Just say he looked peaceful
with his lip partially restored. Just say
they make a special coffin draped in powder blue
for boys, and I learned the name
of a type of bloom: baby's breath.

Christmas went. Rains came hard that winter.
For two months I tracked down the missing
gravestone. Dying is business too.
Mistakes occur. You never asked me
about the search. If I found anything,
you figured, I'd let you know. I did,

locating the marker in the cemetery
stockyard's maze of grief, after sifting
among the "beloved," "adored," "devoted,"
and other titles of the dead,
sifting through promises to "meet again."

So, months later was the ground re-stirred,
I almost said re-christened, and
the remains officially named.

8
A Photo

Even now to watch parents guard an empty crib,
if only in the shelter of imagination,

tests my endurance. For weeks I played
the portable night long, and when

the station signed off, its snow and static
wept into my dreams. Here were sounds

suppressing absence, incoherent
light sustaining incoherent sleep.

My sister mailed a *Newsweek*
entitled "When Parents Lose a Child."

A forlorn photo showed a man grieving.
Below, the caption: *When is it my turn*

to cry? My turn came. The night
you held me, rocked me tight,

tighter, to squeeze my pent-up
sorrow into your embrace, until

in a fleeting moment of our solitude
we shared a single breaking heart.

9
How It Was

Rising early into the dawn's promise,
the bride asked why he stole his body

to her side of the bed, why he placed his face
to her pillow's retreating warmth. Wasn't

it love enough to make love, to share sheets,
dinners, dishes, towels, the same spent rug?

She remembers camping in the Northwest.
Driving 600 miles a day. To pitch camp,

cook, clean, sleep, break camp and set off
the next a.m. In Yakima they'd had enough

and tried a motel. Just twenty dollars.
They hauled out the Coleman and grilled burgers

in a local park. Like regency. Outside Spokane,
they camped at a local KOA, barely feet

from neighbors on each side.
Still they made love, it was hard

and eager, in the dark, and then
they did it again.

*   *   *

I am at the house to visit the children.
Almost grown, they are frequently out.
I spoon food to the cat, step outside
and rough the dog's loyal flanks
as it shoves its neighborly snout
in my direction. For a while I'll catch
some television. You've retreated upstairs
to a variety special or Movie of the Week.
It's quiet. The crickets chirp. The dog
barely stirs, and sometimes the cat pads about,
as if summoning memory of the predator it dreams
it was. It joins me in a yawn. It's then
it wants to slip out the side door, softly,
the way shade melts into greater shade,

without so much as a sound.

Part 4:
Hoy Sum Means Happy

The Problem of Radiance

Radiance nervously ascends the stairs.
At the top a door waits among multiple perturbations.

The door has changing proportions
that redistribute the weight of doubt.

Or maybe these are stars not stairs
to mount, and a door in motion

with impatient thoughts and no conclusions
fails to wait. You see the problem

proportion claims. You contemplate
the perturbations of stars.

Tactile Narrative

I remember my hand working
its shape into yours
that first night of café romance.
If you don't recall, never mind.
But the meeting of hands was a thrill,
the light points of pressure spreading
in an arc I'll resist calling a heartbeat
this time only. What surprised me
were the lines madly crisscrossing
your palms like routes gone haywire
on a travel map. As if a surplus
of possibilities had met,
quarreled and staggered off
in opposing directions.
We had been speaking of your life.
The waiters scurried back and forth,
occasionally pecking at our table,
thinking to liberate it for
the next set of words.
I was thinking my future is here.
You said *I hate my hands.*

Sunday

My phone has lost its will to live.
A rose blushes in a crystal vase,
repeats its pattern in a dishtowel
old with spills. Last night

I felt the pull in you of obligation.
If only you had let our knees
brush tenderly where we sat,
our hands twine soft as petals,

as vows, I could have surprised you
with a lyric disguised as a rose.
Why am I always caught off guard
when feelings change? How

should I try this knowledge, redeem
this absence, or manage at letting go?

Open Heart

In Cantonese hoy sum
open heart
means *happy*.

Working the crossword in bed
I track six letters as clue.
They part at the center.

Buried in my chest is
an artery
for the words that hurt
to hurtle through

for the aching blood
to wake to its new
vocabulary.

Inside my chest is a gate
you once passed through.
You fumbled protectively
for a latch.

I thought I mentioned
before you left
there are no words for how
you make me feel

or did I say there is no
latch on happiness
neither coming

nor going.

Winchell's, 12:05 a.m.

The conversation pitches
back and forth across an aisle.
Wads of money appear to be at stake.

I won't rush my cinnamon roll.
But you could call this a bad night

for the guy beneath the baseball cap
who folds and unfolds his 7 Up
like an aluminum dollar bill.
Is it pain, I wonder,
or booze that's got him by the balls
as he staggers off to fetch
his wash next door? With me

it's a peculiar taste for hanging on
too hard too long. May I get personal?

I can't sleep and appetite's the thing
I can't let go of
or even share without
you here. If only

it were you and not the night manager
stirring batter through
that tin contraption rigged
for squeezing zeroes into oil—so
that's how it's done, how it's done, how it's done.

The Sanity of Tomatoes

1.

Tomatoes are not a poignant fruit,
not with their wide, affable faces,
their compliances with the eager knife.
They recline in slices on the cutting board,
all their operations a success.

Their miniatures pose shinily in salad bowls,
beaded with moisture, bathed in exotic dressings.
When you bite them whole, they squeal in delight.
They squirt your teeth with their mad rejoicings.

I've seen them, jolted off the tops of overloaded trucks,
careening excitedly down empty stretches of highway,
not looking where they go, never signaling,
indifferent to pebbled roadskin and ditch and the deadly
asseverations of trucks with their redundant 18 wheels.
Ah, lending needed color to the landscape.

2.

But I know when I hold the tomato at eye level,
it reminds you of an asymmetrical heart.
Reminds you of an undiscovered bruise—
elastic skin, the grace of the tongue
tasting the fruit that copies the heart
that navigates your world.

Consider two tomatoes in love.
How can they kiss?
How can she hold him in her arms?
How can they whisper the forbidden words?

They knock their heads together,
their skins, their shiny red butts.
You make your vow, and the tomatoes sing.

3.

When I think of tomatoes I see the phalanxes of plants
once guarding the plains of Ventura and Oxnard,
and hands picking tomatoes,
the ones the harvester missed with its complicated gears and blades.

Tough and raw, unburnished pelt,
those hands aren't soft with condescension,
not shaped to wield a pen alone, or deliberate.

Having warred with brambles, burrs, aphids,
having browned with the faces of pinoys and braceros,
they grip the green and ripening youth
and the yellow and red maturity
with the alacrity of the initiated.

The tomatoes never flinch.
They never shout in hoarse voices at the lack of tenderness.
They are grateful for the one hand reaching out,
left or right, it makes no difference,

and they take the hand,
and inside the curl of it they place the moment.

This is the sanity of tomatoes.

On an Impending Wedding

Tonight I won't steer this poem past some local haunt.
Or if I do, I'll place another couple inside it,
not ourselves. Have her drive. Let the man

glance her way, keeping his thoughts to himself.
The headlights shining boastfully, the poem
chases their beam, and the road unfurls

like a trail of expectations. Behind her lies
nothing that matters. Then a flickering,
the headlights dim and stutter, they shut off

on their own accord. I like that word, accord,
it's even better in the dark. I didn't say this couple
was in love, did I? Good. It's hard enough

to maneuver poems without jealousy butting in.
Accord is sufficient. Now she taps her fingers
on the wheel. Not that she's cross

but there's a tune playing in her head.
Her tapping makes the man like her even more.
Have I made myself clear? She has a knack

for making men answer her smallest actions
with their hearts. I won't pretend this poem
corners, accelerates, handles like no other,

but a consummation is at hand, and a need
to bear witness. Years later some lights snap on.
She faces him, wondering about the random

turns a poem takes. I don't claim she thinks
about someone else. I just say she reflects
on the road's oddities and imperfections. Maybe

the man has troubled himself with similar reflections.
If so, I won't report them. It's not his poem.
Despite his occupying the best seat in it.

Historical Sequence for Wan-Hsin

1
On Being Separated

Two more months! Months!
I will divide them into shapes of cut pears.
Without cores and stems, they will feed my waiting.
So delicious to the tongue, so hard a loss to bear.

2
In the Lilac Park

Amazing how the mulberry spreads its trunk
so lovers can lean in its embrace. How the biker
whirrs by, clicking her gears at the next uphill.
As an elderly man in hat and suspenders chases a dog with his eyes

before inspecting his pocketwatch a second time.
How the children in strollers glide past the important grandstand.
How the soccer ball bounces off in wayward pleasure
and the walkway curves gracefully towards the practice field,

where the bat strikes the ball with a convincing *crack*.
Amazing how lovers fail to notice any of this.
But holding hands and occasionally kissing,
they obey every park rule on the proper exercise of time.

3
Terminus: After the Fortune Teller

Tonight I am utterly alone with thoughts of you,
shimmering as embers. I throw open my window
to cool them in the moon's celestial basin.
Emerging, they glisten preciously into stars.
Are these thoughts mute with remembered rapture,
or can they fly into eloquence, even
as dusk deliberates over Taipei and Touliu?

The blade of mortality cuts harshly
at the night's tranquil skin.
I will calm those wounds with the aloe
of human breathing in a bed after love.
Do you remember our passionate intensity?
Our deepest cries and longing
for the core of each other's virtuous heart?

Tonight I am utterly alone except
for the world pulsing outside my window,
of which the swallow's silent inhabitation of grief
and the cricket's melodious protest of dawn
are sign
          like the fragments of heaven,
beloved Hsin, still portioned to you and to me.

Dining on Poetry in Little Taipei

Tonight I find my poem in the noodle shop.
The mild din clears, families depart.
The chatter of college students on a food run
follows them to and from their automobiles,
until it too, played out, rises to leave.

I'd like to snatch a piece
of Mandarin irony and eat it
in this Hong Kong-style café,
as a wedge of lemon looks expectantly on,
as the soy hovers at the edge of a taste bud
known less for wisdom than susceptibility to wit.
Make me laugh. Let me dine on laughter,
curried ox tongue, and forget-me-nots.

My glance dives through the doors of the kitchen,
then lands on its feet before the cook,
whose hands are supple as the noodles he kneads and quilts,
suave as the cleaver that *k-chonks!* the duck.
The burner gasps once, fires, and the meat sizzles,
the snow peas blink in a surf of sesame oil.
Winsome sleds of onion ride a cutting board,
navigate grave forests of gai lan.
Rafts of bell pepper dip and bob in a pan
as cubes of pineapple lounge in bowls,
their smart tongues ready with quips.

It is late when I find my poem sitting on a plate,
the room free of all disturbance but me,
and in this delicious loneliness of existence
we prepare to speak.

(Monterey Park, California)

As for This

Age matters. Like rivets
on a bridge you think will last.

Age and the direction the will takes
no longer subject to maniacal storms.

That's why my answers sound like rust.
Even in the dwindling conversation, your kiss

is the one my lips want to remember.
If the fog fails to lift, I'll settle for less.

Reading Poems Written by Others

I love the ones so full of nails bristling in the hemlock
of an old unreconciled wound geez the hurt in that life
makes you want to lie down in snow and shut your eyes
like a tired cow. But I mean the ones swinging, sure, on grief
that ploop! turn around just as your attention threatens to wane.
I mean the ones that all of a sudden hitch up their pants,
slip on some high-heeled boots, pomade their renegade hair,
and stride out the door without locking it or looking back
because, shoot, they know everything worth keeping
is with them right now, and the night, boys, the night is young.

Essay on History and Persiflage

1
Oakland

Waterside in the East Bay bistro, they
chart the sun's decline into May,

tilting a month's last wages on roofs of the city.
They toast its munificence at a window

with a sculpted view. The room
mimics tradition with a cautious grace,

the way one says demitasse,
as if the word itself might break.

They talk books. She'll praise his tie. Promise
him half her glass of Chardonnay. But no,

already the heads of goblets nod above the bar
at the aureola shimmering from an alcove lamp,

and bric-a-brac misbehave along a wall.
Silently, he calculates his distance from

her voice, his knee from hers.
Sharing plates, they consume

that distance bite by bite. His head
spins. Later he betrays. But first

they invite the waitress into its scent.
First comes appetite and the random

clatter of forks and spoons.

2
Molière on the Gold Coast

The Learned Ladies is minor ore
extracted with arduous wit.

But holding hands excites the nerves.
He feels the magnetic pulse,

pull of tides, the strain of surf
towards strand, and out again,

voluptuously. What time it is
when laughs conclude, applause

dies down, lights come up,
and voices spring into chill night air

he scarcely knows. Nor craves a
second course of Chrysale, Armande et

Henriette, whose antic remoulade was
fit for paste. In the garage's

depths his fond Toyota plays
hide and seek. They search

deliberately enough. Hands embrace.

3
Late Night

He wants to touch her face
before they kiss.

    When at last they
shed the coffee house, the chairs
surmount their tables. The throats
of taps and faucets shut,
while an eerie emptiness
patrols the Berkeley streets.
       Beneath
Orion all commerce goes to bed.

Reaching through the car's dark,
they breathe intimate facts of being
into life.
    What is finally worse?
To traffic deliberately in the moment's
flesh or to insult the hearts'
divulgences in time to come?

Of course. The latter.

      Of course.

For nothing, not the bodies' pre-
dawn hold and clutch (goodbye for now!),
goes deeper than the knowing given
and received, no strings attached,
as gifts.

4
Mendacity

Looking back,
she must ask, why did he not take
a razor to her trust, his doubled
       tongue, even then?

Or in the ensuing
months of tender hopes penned
one by one from that lucid
       start?

She wrote to
ask where he wished to go from here.
He told a truth converted later
       into lie.

It was truth first,
then double-talk, like flame smothered
by self-regarding swirls of smoke.
       Even then

it smoldered on,
relit, and burst outrageously
across a continent. But by then
       the house

of hope
they'd built was gone. A coward's ruin.
Once he was true. Whose line was
       that?

5
Sacred Heart

Then false. When she arrives
in Paris, the Frenchmen find her alluring,
exotic. Of this he is sure. One swears
he would fall upon his sword for her,
la femme savante. Swears with his stare.
She has just met the concierge,
a no-nonsense Briton, so she politely
laughs behind the shield of her propriety.

How does one guess? The blood's an impeccable
source. In the shade of the Basilique
du Sacré Coeur it flows, as she gazes from
a window. She is constant. Like her
degree of caution before the red-faced man.

As if in excuse of the excuse,
one finally mails, in the depths of summer's
swelter. Being wiser, she cuts swiftly

through such self-deceit. His lies topple,
not one maintains its balance. Each hour
he wants to crawl into an explanation
fortified with cause.

A sage, the bookseller announces the text:
tout comprendre, c'est tout pardonner.

Seizing the obvious,
he cries *merci,*

until a voice replies, *tout pardonner,*
c'est rien comprendre.

6
Office Mail

Her final letter is typed.
Its cold recoil from the memories
he preserves shatters his make-believe.

7
Death of Innocence

Weeks later he runs over a cat.
It sits away from the gutters
in the center of the shocked lane,
drenched by rain and drained of precaution.
He catches its stare in the headlights
too late, swerves to straddle
its sudden crouch but hears its
death sicken against the chassis
as he sweeps over. Round and round
he circles, searching for the corpse.
Somehow it has reached a final bower
or gained a familiar porch.
Or the force of impact has carried it
fifty feet beyond his futile search.

In the rear-view
a middle-aged man sobs into his chest.
But the cat can't care.

8
Medicinal

He won't be healed by remorse.
Gram by gram,
he swallows these words until

their comfort dissolves, the wound
reopens, the ache reappears,

and he is again undeceived.

The prescription:
Take many times daily.
Exceeding the maximum dose.

Part 5:
Giving Up the Elements

Dining with the Saltmans
at Rivoli, North of Berkeley

Sweet cream of corn soup,
shrimp and clam couscous,

and a raspberry shortcake
with three pecking forks

to wind our evening down. . .
Outside the picture window

six raccoons come to the feeder.
I watch the juveniles fail

to cavort like comic bandits
impersonating their masks.

Anyway, the leukemia tires Ben.
Helen knows when to call it quits.

She's seen them all before,
the raccoons, the skunks in pairs,

knows there's nothing to feed them
from behind this shield of glass

but her quiet, divided attention.
I'm talking about their bashful

beating hearts, the matchless
ease with which their delible

lives proceed.

(In memory of Benjamin Saltman)

Wisdom

Someone lugs a watermelon, thumps it, listens.
Later, as a blade stands above its ribs,

pausing surgically, I recall my ex father-in-law—
bus mechanic and handyman, used car sales
washout, animal show devotee, plaid-shirted grounds-

keeper & provost of watermelons. A backyard man
pirating a cigarette in a viney retreat.
Sunk in the plush of tomato prosperity.
As nearby the portable revved with Indy or Daytona.

They say wisdom holds its tongue,
bares its wings.
If so, add another excellence to his resumé.
Dub him the golden monarch.

To one of his daughters he imparted
his own habits of silence, which she accepted
with the same comfortable consistency I never grasped.

I think when he greeted a watermelon, his listening
lay in the fingers, the meditating palm.

Somehow his grandchildren
caught on to the tender inquisition,
which was watermelon-deep, rind-simple.

Now both cherish the echo of the watermelon,
though neither desires the fruit. So, listening with care,

you can still hear the analogy of a heart:
quiet man, watermelon man.

Unrequited Love: An Essay on Identity, or What Went Wrong, Suzy Wong?

What can I wear to please you at last?
An epicanthic fold across a staged reaction,

or something small as a crease in my self-esteem,
abetted by surgery & American TV?

Shall an imperial flag bind my feet?
The slave takes mincing, mincing steps.

To the harbor she goes, dutiful beggar
to the rich man who owns the past.

What can be done to make you stay?
If I satisfy this thirst of the senses

for the rosemary touch, scent, persimmon mouth,
agile hips, the play of mysterious words in the dark,

will you honor my every request?
If I bring you books, provocative hours

of thought, feelings disguised as maxims
from the Orient, will you unveil your secrets?

Dear one, let us read from an authentic text,
let us mingle our sacred breaths.

My whole life I have loved without possessing you,
spectre, elusive ghost, changeling, my torment—

even now I feel the subtle churnings of the heart.
Intemperately, the turnings of the tide.

Teaching the Stroke Victim

I try to teach you to speak.
You in your pajamas wrongly buttoned,
your face dirty with beard, listen. The tongue
is your oar, its rowing constant,
the labials poof or hum, depending.
And the dentals, well, you must remember
those infamous pliers from school.
The last time I let you fix my teeth,
you drilled without a local, the repair being
so minor and I being your son.
Now we talk. Your sounds are rudderless,
they grope for an invisible shore of sense.
The chest wheezes with frustration
at the violent intimacy of language and being.
Now we ease our way back to beginnings.

Today I open my book and the word is *patience*,
a soft word, a lost art. That time
at the kitchen table when I lost mine
and you started to sob never quite
leaves me. Twelve years after your death,
I hear you sounding out the easy vowels,
I think of sons who make their fathers cry.

The Riddle

A pair of nightwatchmen talked idly by a doorway.
A man lay somewhere deep in its shadows.
A siren died blocks away on the lesser hills,
lest sleep in its quiet brimming be spilt,
when, gliding brilliantly underground,
Hope and its urgent attendants should arrive.
But this man lay soiled in his bedclothes.
He longed to undo his sheets, undo
the baffling knots flesh winds itself in,
and free the soul, if there was one, to perform
its last ragged stunt before the disbeliever
Night, leaning in enormously at the window.

Elsewhere the newborns slept and cried and slept.
Activity slowed but never ceased around this paradox.
The ambulance stood motionless in its stall,
its motor still running like the imaginary
hum of the earth before daybreak.
Even the man finally yawned and scratched himself,
then twisted his body toward sleep.
You could read the body's "s" by the nightlamp.
In fact from each window a light glimmered.
Light was stacked on light, row on row,
like a riddle holding the darkness up,
or a shuttle of well-wishers at a funeral
one by one struck dumb with wonder.

Giving Up the Elements

Giving up the impartial atoms,
the colliding logic you were rooted in,
giving up the earth's brown rods,
morning at the first pitch
of light, giving up the tilted
molecules, the calculus of risk
increase, decrease, joy, dismay,
the hot heart of the sun, the hole
it burns in the entropic air,
air stubbled with fire like
the hot lake of the heart,
giving up health, giving up hope,
giving up the last gust
of hope, the last ghost
of a chance, giving up chance

where it bloomed on its single stem.

Elegy at Church of the Hills

(for Hae Won Park, 32)

If last night was tropical in L.A. and today it's the dry,
desert variety of July, does earth decelerate at the rate

we start to do? Heat breeds reluctance, true. And that's
one good reason movement slows as it nears the tidy chapel,

but just one. Only weeks ago you were active,
plagued you thought by an ulcer, the type of wound

the epithelium won't tolerate without complaint. But
malignancy is a thief. It steals you the instant

the future turns its back. Meanwhile, the rest of your life
waits for you to catch up, as relaxed as the eucalyptus

gracing a lawn, idling in place. This church, erected
on nothing more than recrudescent faith, circa 1740,

near the height of the Great Awakening, is an idea
stolen from New England, okay. But at worst that's commerce

at Forest Lawn, the importation of a salt-weathered fib
to an arid clime. You'd have laughed at the novelty,

having a sharp eye for cultural confusions and not just
because you were born in Seoul. To repeat,

I can't make sense of this senseless code or finger
a guilty party. Your classrooms await you in the fall,

somnolent as heat. Your students, untested, dry as tinder,
want igniting with a Promethean sort of flame. So there's

another myth beneath this big broad sun. Inside,
this solemn vestibule's invitingly picturesque

and mercifully cool. But even it can't ignore those sobs
already racking the sanctuary. Hae Won, those are sounds

of disbelieving hearts. Staying awake but mortally slow.

Aging

When your neighbor's daughter drops by
to borrow flour, suddenly you're happy as snow.

Being young is a disadvantage. But to want
one neighborly thing and to get it with ease

reassures you. The road narrows. It shortens.
There comes the point when everything else

seems trivial, everything except the frail reaching out,
why, we are less durable than snowflakes—

that helps you go from here to there.

Autumnal

(for Janice Ono, 1945–1995)

Labor Day, 1977

Nadine takes the slide backwards to startle the pool.
Thirteen, she mimics a seal, as she aims
her confidence over the slide's hump
toward a plush wet welcome,
$\qquad\qquad\qquad$ sure as mother-love.

Allen works the grill: hot dogs gain their stripes,
flagrantly split their toes. Burgers pop
and sizzle on their pink, onion-lit bellies, pop-
POP! as steaks exhale, take heed of flame
and edge past rare. Nothing's so rare
in the aquamarine pace of the holiday
as the splash of hurry.
$\qquad\qquad\qquad$ Even the crowd swells
with effort. Kids turn and brown in the sun.
The boys wanting to follow Nadine's lead
and being boys afraid to show
they're afraid, wait warily.
$\qquad\qquad\qquad$ The aunties
peck at scraps of gossip, the men load up
on relaxation, their talk free flows
toward fellowship, and when the booze spills,
they watch their feet out of the way,
while one hunts up the paper towels

that materialize with you, having checked
the oven, cracked the watermelon, sliced the pies,

found and flung the car keys, and squeezed
fresh lemonade from fruit off Uncle's tree.
You are everywhere the laughter is,

                              your subtle,
straight-faced punch lines break us up,
your welcome pairs the glide toward dusk.

Outside, beneath your glance,
the boys like slim torpedoes

                        careen and plunge.

At Kaiser Permanente

It feels like I'm not here. Enmeshed in tubes,
thick with edema, you lend this remark an air

of surprise. As if presence were first
to slip away, wraith-like, while the body

lags behind, uninformed, grazing on morphine.
Behind your bed's a wall bearing a clock

that is not a clock, whose hands point dumbly
at the flux of health. What can they tell us

that your mother's hands knitting something
together stitch by hopeless stitch

in the waiting room cannot say? Do they relieve
pain, dress wounds, lend succor, stir laughter

like you? Even now, as your tongue rolls
the shapes of words, we all lean closer to catch

a taste: some breezy reflection, hilarious bon mot.
Something of your life has entered us drop by drop.

This is the way of nourishment that seeks
to visit the veins though the veins contract

in sorrow and regret. They feel peculiar too,
those counting the minutes one by one,

                                        who feel
for all the world that you're not here.

Requiem

Your fellow nurses click slides
you have helped select.
In the background Satchmo
serenades your baby pictures,
shots with family,
the Peter Pan collars
of your white blouse school days,
candids at work
to make the mourners smile,

and on the upbeat
Aretha demands r-e-s-p-e-c-t

Part 6:
Disorient Ballroom

After the Dance I Benefit
from Good Advice Given Over the Phone

she says to write a happy poem
something so very outstanding
then she says *go to sleep*
as she did a little girl in shanghai
in the family's one bed
with her mother   her father
away somewhere maybe in hong kong
she never complains about being poor
tells me again to write a happy poem

Learning English

Newly wed, you scan the TV
as baby grows and grows inside
like a tumult of days.
You've cleaned the apartment,
you know no one in this place.
For now the Americans scamper
down the aisle, waving tags or numbers,
knowing indeed *The Price Is Right.*

Your head tallies the differentials
faster than the numbers turn. You
watch intently as glee rises, and falls,
and rises, and furniture and appliances,
and wardrobes and *aiyaa!*
the brand new fully equipped,
fully automatic, air-conditioned,
bucket-seated, tinted-windowed jackpots
take their bold stand. Except

along with the dream of being
that Lucky Someone
whose front door prosperity
suddenly knock-knocks at,
you are rolling the shapes of America
on your tongue and in your mouth.
Congratulations! you say,
when you greet husband at the door.
Too bad! as you serve
the pleasing evening meal.
The man looks at you in a puzzled way.

Though he's proud of his smart, capable wife,
he little imagines the other courses
still to come: *Three's Company,*
Lucy, and *The Brady Bunch.*

Your Teenage Fury Is a Blind Arrow

Hurtling down the 605,
for a moment we draw alongside an eighteen-wheeler.
I realize your anger might pull us hard right
and out of this world of harsh feelings.

I keep humming a Strauss waltz,
having recently learned to dance
and grown calmer since the divorce.

You tell me this secret.
That on summer camps, trips away from home,
the only person you ever missed
was Grandpa Mike.

I keep humming the waltz.
But I think about the mangled bodies
beneath the frozen wreckage.
Not me. Not even Mom.

How Am I Driving?
I can't say right now, truck.
I am holding on to a secret
I myself haven't learned to steer.

Aubade

Suppose you waken one morning and the person
beside you has changed names. You call her *Waltz*.
Now every previous day of your life secedes
from memory. Your bank account is empty,
empty as a nation that has lost its states.
Only the numbers give a clue to your missing identity.
Or you reach for the coffee beans: French Roast or *Rumba*.
You move your ribs to the thick slow brew, four-and-one,
the daylight breaking, two-three. You catch a face
in a mirror, the razor scratching shadows
percussively. Readying for work, you cannot recall
what you do or the road that gets you there.
Your heart cranks up to a syncopated *cha-and-cha*,
and you sense the day gathering momentum
outside your frame of reference. All you know
is contained in a closed promenade. That's it.
Tango. The last you recall from the night before,
before your fate went blind to the prospect of light.

The Waltz Is

revenge. Pull up,
No, *pull up* from the waist
without straightening the knees.
Especially the buttocks, lose them.
Elongate that tepid wire, your spine.
Lengthen the lilt of
your neck. Tighten
the abdomen where
the calories hang out,
suck in those hips, now
press *down* from the shoulders
as you press *up* through the sides.
Don't think to ask gravity
for an opinion. In fact,
don't think. The neck
pearls to the left, the head
lightens, the eyes appear to
glaze, this is not
a staring match, *stop*
whining, please.
Offer the left hand,
folding the fingers so,
the hint of pressure
in the middle ones alone.
Elbows up!
And when
the hips
and only when
they nearly kiss outright,
cup your right hand
to the shoulder blade

or a fraction below,
fingers together like an oar.
Let partner's hand settle
to complete the frame.
Never lose this frame.
Do not turn your head, dip
your hands, bounce your shoulders,
drop your elbows,
relax your middle,
lose your timing or bother
to breathe.
Now you are ready
for the first step.

Listen, Foxtrot

you false front of jaunty jalopiness,
cool cruiser down the avenue of stars,
you light-legged *lippity-lippity*, sentimentaled
stroll through the meandersome
green-laced, wood-thatched perennial park,
you can't con me with your slow-slow,
quick-quick rest-easy trot-trot walkalong gait
or swell serendipity. Oh no. I know your kind
of reputation for good will and social charity.
But I see the shadow that shadows your steps.
I limn the slow-quick-quick of your true pulse.
Surely it is lightness of an inside edge
aspired to in vain, or flawless weave
to the feather finish. The telemark's lilt
at the tail of count two is metaphor for hope
that the heel, heel-toe, toe-heel of a three-step
softly tramples. The chassé's easeful
syncopations proclaim progress is at hand,
but the reverse check's deception
restores the suspense. Oh, bittersweet
tantalizer, long-stepped promise, again
you tempt us across the bedizened floor
we heel-turn so nearly neatly on.

Disorient Ballroom

The British codified the rules, became the best practitioners,
along with their descendants. The world flocks to Blackpool.

Germans, Italians, French. The Americans, Canadians, and Finns.
The Japanese as a contingent, mainland Chinese in observance,

their finest preparing for the Olympics. In Los Angeles I dance
on Thursday nights. Lessons on Mondays, Wednesdays, Saturdays.

In Los Angeles I dance on Sunday nights. Lesson on Tuesday
          mornings.
At the studios are Asians, most are middle-aged or beyond.

From Nanjing, Hong Kong, Taipei. From Diamond Bar via Seoul.
From West L.A. via Manzanar, Monterey Park via Poston AZ.

From Bangkok, Manila, Singapore. From Ho Chi Minh City
and the scarred lands beyond. Some practice the rules of

international dance set out by the British and observed at Blackpool.
They don't go there, aiming to compete. But stay here, at home,

altering local images of the ballroom and the dance, fervent
as warriors as revolutionaries plotting their next unprecedented move.

Cultural Intervention

The ballroom fills
with asians who
perform the asiantine tango
the rumba de la asian amor
the asia quickstep
with charleston styling
plus step-hops
a la asiénne
who dig the jive
the jitterbug and
asian lindy
but swirl to the asianese waltz
both quick and slow
and snap and snap
the cha-and-asian-cha
brave the syncopats
of the brazilasian samba
and mount the foxtrot's
asian astaire way to heaven.

Cuban Breaks

2-and-3 (and) 4-and-1
2-and-3 (and) 4-and-1
now do new yorkers syncopate
quick-and-quick
quick-and-quick
and hit the spot turn
extra spin
to hand-to-hand
and rock and rock uh! 4
and spot and cha-cha-1
heyjump!
and lock-and-lock
uh-rondé-ooh! and
lock-and-lock uh-rondé-2
forward back
and lock-and-lock uh-rondé-3
and lock-and-1-(and)-2-
(and) rockstep-backstep-lock-and-1
natural tops plus spiral spiral
open out add hip twist—
FAN! to allemagne
bring it home and start again
(lordy lordy)
cubanbreaks cubanbreaks

Dance for the Vietnamese Diaspora

I send myself across waters of vicissitude
from the grip of a monsoon,

in the belly of a boat,
on the pleadings of wind.

Above me a cloud bursts drunkenly into tears.
Why are you sad, little mood?

Today is filled with importance.
My father's hopes chew fervently on the bit,

they stamp their intrepid hooves. Forward,
to the lading dock where the amber glows,

where the America of the blood
pounds its distant steady beat, beat!

Today we commemorate the expenditures of hope,
as the lumbering beast of language snores,

as tomorrow's squalid truths recede
from evening's dimpled rim.

Fear not the destination,
children of the river crossing,

O gallant pioneers.
Ahead the driest spot on earth,

your destiny: a place
neither here, nor home.

Valse Triste

My poor feet understand the music.
Just one moment,
while I credit my feet.

How they heel, toe, toe-heel
us into a corner and spin-turn us
out. My feet are my own

village, they fill with movement,
private thoughts, big plans.
Such cleverness, such risk.

Whisk! And wing to chassé
and an outside change. My feet
are brave paddles, the floor

a river of tears. Because
complications occur.
So a quick open reverse

to challenge line and oversway.
Or make it a throwaway
because in ballroom it's beautiful

to throw away. My feet are truth,
hop aboard. Hop aboard
these fraternal twins

as they reverse slip pivot,
double reverse to *bombshell*,
slip and contra, and start again.

It's sad, *mes amis*.
Or else it is not beautiful,
merely routine. So never forget

the trace in each figure.
Watch! As my feet hover telemark,
it's subtle as one, two, and-three.

Taking an Inside Edge

Watching you dance. Watching your life
follow the invisible track of polished floor
and take an angle on an inside edge,
I know why you told me *reality is terrible*.
My fate can't agree. But I enjoin it
to watch as you deliver your conviction
diagonally center, diagonally wall,
in the body's subtle mission. Quiet rise.
Quiet fall. Resplendent in your gown, ·
you catch the admiring glances. Odd
how the jaded pro executes each figure
without sensing the heart beating in his arms.
Heart suffering reality. Its opposite projected
irreducibly along a simple line of dance.

Gift

I have settled on the necklace.
But would rather give you a dance.
A dance so elegant you could wear it
to the finest restaurants and hotels. A dance
so dazzling it would be viewed nightly
in theatres, in supper clubs, and on cable TV,
where the audiences would exclaim,
"however did you get such a beautiful dance?"

A dance so intimate you could wear it to bed,
dreaming it, and in the morning brush your teeth,
the dance still alive in your mouth.
I would rather give you a dance so perfect
that were eternity a polished floor,
it would be dedicated forever to your dance,
and yours alone. Instead I offer this necklace,
which is purchasable gold, and within explanation.

Watching Dancers
at the Senior Center

Without suffering there is no dance.
Likewise there is no fiction
without the prospect of age

or infirmity. But they don't look
infirm and you'd have to read
between the lines to detect pain

beyond the hardship of the next new step.
There are no sermons without condescension.
No favors without a rip someplace

in the heart, as you don't need
to be told. So mum's the word.
When the shoes shuffle

across the floor I detect whispers.
When the knees knockety-knock
I see they're close

to the undisheveled instant
when the dance tells its story
like no other you have ever heard.

How What Comes to Happen
Comes to Pass

It's obvious the evening loves me.
Under this air, even the coffin
looks unremarkable,
a splinter of wood,
waiting. Under this eave,
the day's minor disruptions depart,
the insults that seemed so costly
scatter like the unraked leaves
resembling moths' wings
that hover and dart in the gusts,
yesterday, today,
name it, let it.
For the millions
to whom each day is harsh,
this evening may be no different
from the rest, reminding
them only of their fatigue,
despair, or unaltered fates.
If I wish this evening were
the sleek fur of a dog or cat
I could mold comfortingly
to your touch, if I wish
it were a sack of money
of such largesse it paid interest
on your fears and alarms
and the sickening realization
that your plan is not working,
if I wish it were a performance
so superior you were transported
to a realm ineffable and just, you

might take one step back to the dawn
where your first light began,
where your knocking resembled
the waking of wood,
and your infant weight,
though it changes nothing,
seemed lighter than air.

Glossary

bakatare—stupid, stupid idiot

bracero—esrtwhile term for Mexican agricultural laborers

Ehime—Japanese prefecture

Heart Mountain—World War II Japanese American internment camp in Wyoming

Hele mai—come here (Hawaiian)

tout comprendre, c'est tout pardonner—to understand all is to forgive all (proverbial)

tout pardonner, c'est rien comprendre—to forgive all is to understand nothing (proverbial)

Little Taipei—erstwhile designation for Monterey Park, California, by Taiwanese immigrants in the mid-1980s

messu haru—corruption of "mess hall"

Minidoka—World War II Japanese American internment camp in Idaho

nisei—second-generation Japanese Americans

ofuro—bath

otomodachi—friend

pinoys—vernacular form for Filipino countrymen or countrywomen (especially pinays) developed in the U.S.

Shikoku—one of Japan's four main islands

Touliu—city in Taiwan

tsuma—wife

yaoya—green grocer, green grocery

George Uba was born in Chicago, Illinois. A literary critic, writer, and professor, he currently serves as chair of the English Department at California State University, Northridge. He has been an amateur international-style ballroom dancer for eight years.

Printed in the United States
21566LVS00001B/361-411